KT-558-064

INCHLEY

All About
Muscles

by Anne Giulieri

30131 05530729 9

LONDON BOROUGH OF BARNET

a Capstone company — publishers for children

Engage Literacy is published in the UK by Raintree.
Raintree is an imprint of Capstone Global Library Limited, a company incorporated in England and Wales having its registered office at 264 Banbury Road, Oxford, OX2 7DY – Registered company number: 6695582

www.raintree.co.uk

© 2017 by Raintree. All rights reserved. No part of this publication may be reproduced, stored in a retrieval system, or transmitted in any way or by any means, electronic, mechanical, photocopying, recording or otherwise, without the prior written permission of Capstone Global Library Limited.

Text copyright © Anne Guilieri 2017

Editorial credits
Jennifer Huston, editor; Richard Parker, designer; Pam Mitsakos, media researcher; Katy LaVigne, production specialist

Image credits
Getty Images: SHUBHANGI GANESHRAO KENE, 6 bottom left inset, Yukmin, 5; iStockphoto: isitsharp, 15, princigalli, 22; Science Source: BSIP, 6 right, 17; Shutterstock: 3445128471, 9 bottom left, Africa Studio, 19, carballo, 8, Cover shop, design element, Daniel Jedzura, 16, Elina Manninen, 20, Ilya Andriyanov 4, Jesse Kunerth, 23, Max Topchii, 10, Monkey Business Images, 13 bottom, 21, naluwan, 18, Sadovnikova Olga, 14, Samuel Borges Photography, 9 top right, snapgalleria, 13 top, TinnaPong, 11; Thinkstock: Brand X Pictures, 7, David De Lossy, back cover, Todd Warnock, cover

Glossary
Shutterstock: ankomando, (breath), BlueRingMedia, (adult), (blood), (stairs), Fun Way Illustration, (muscles), GraphicsRF, (exercise), Linusy, (bunch), Lorelyn Medina (humans), Meganeura, (blink), omnimoney, (frown), Peter Hermes Furian, (tongue), Yayayoyo, (yawn)

10 9 8 7 6 5 4 3 2 1
Printed and bound in China.

All About Muscles

ISBN: 9781474739276

Contents

The human body

The *human* body is amazing.
It has many different parts
that help to make it work.
All of our body parts are important
because they each do different jobs.

Have you ever wondered how you
walk, run or climb?
Or how you dance, swim or ride a bike?
Special parts inside your body
help you to do these things.
They are called *muscles*.

Muscles

Muscles are soft and red. They look like a *bunch*, or group, of tiny threads put together.

We have lots of different muscles in our bodies. They all have important jobs to do.

Muscles of the Human Body

We use muscles to move our bodies.
Muscles also help us to lift, pull and
push things.
There are even muscles that help to
move things around inside our bodies.

Muscles help us to move

We have about 650 muscles that help us to move and do things.
They help us to sit, walk and stand up tall.
Muscles help us to roll over, *yawn* and *blink* our eyes.

When we smile
we use the muscles
in our faces.

Did you know?

It takes 17 muscles to smile and 43 muscles to *frown!* So it's a lot easier to smile.

Have you ever been swimming, ridden
a bike or climbed across monkey bars?
Have you ever walked up a lot of *stairs*?

When you first started doing these things,
you might have found them difficult.
Your muscles might have hurt
or become tired.

But if you keep doing things over
and over again, they become easier.
That's because the more you
use your muscles, the stronger
they become!

Your muscles can also become
stronger by pushing, pulling
and lifting things.

Muscles move things in the body

Some of our muscles help to move things around inside our bodies.
These muscles make things move by getting tight and then getting loose, or relaxing.

Muscles help to move *blood* around inside our bodies.
They also help to move food through our bodies.
We often don't even notice that these muscles are working!

The Human Digestive System

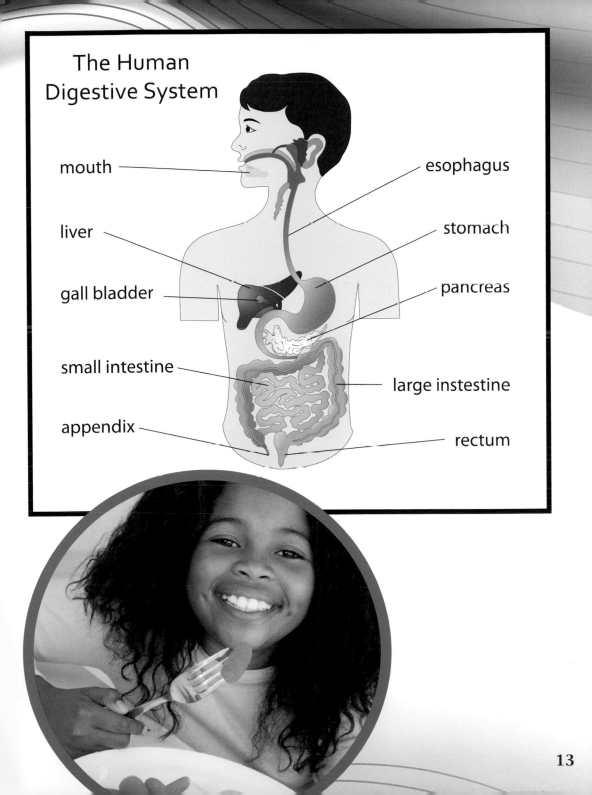

mouth

esophagus

liver

stomach

gall bladder

pancreas

small intestine

large instestine

appendix

rectum

The heart muscle

The heart is a big muscle. This muscle keeps the heart pumping blood through our bodies. The heart muscle does more work than any of our other muscles because it never stops!

To keep your heart healthy, you need lots of *exercise*.

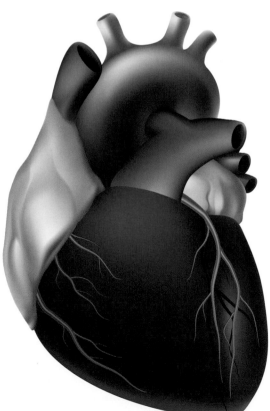

Did you know?

The human heart is about the size of your fist.

You can exercise by running around
with your friends, playing a sport
or even just playing on the playground.

Sometimes when you exercise you can feel
your heart beating really fast.
You might also feel out of *breath*.
There's nothing wrong with that.
The more you exercise, the longer
it will take for you to feel out of breath.

Amazing muscles

There are many muscles
inside our bodies.
They come in many
different shapes and sizes.
Muscles can be small or big.
They can be long, thin or wide.
Some muscles are strong.
No matter their size or shape,
all muscles have important jobs to do.

The stapedius is
the smallest muscle
in the human body.
It is located in the middle ear.

The smallest muscle is inside our ears.
It's smaller than the tip of a pencil.

The longest muscle is very thin.
It goes all the way from the hip
to the knee.

The widest muscle covers the middle
of our backs.
The strongest muscle is the muscle
that helps us to chew.
This muscle helps us to open and close
our mouths.

Did you know?

When babies are born, they have the same muscles as *adults*.
But the muscles are smaller because the babies are not fully grown yet.

Our muscles help us to move and play.
We need to exercise to keep
our muscles healthy and strong.

It is fun to run, swim and play.
All of these exercises help to build
strong muscles.
Healthy muscles are important
for everyone.

Life without muscles

Just imagine if you did not have muscles!
You would not be able to carry
your school bag or play on the playground.
You would not be able to walk, run
or even sit up.
And you would not be able to smile
or chew your food.
So, to work
and play,
we need
our muscles.

Did you know?

The *tongue* has eight muscles.

Picture glossary

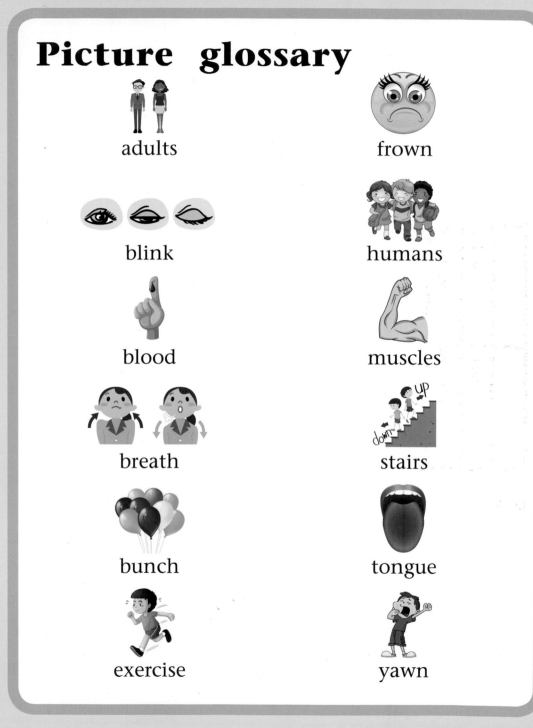

adults

frown

blink

humans

blood

muscles

breath

stairs

bunch

tongue

exercise

yawn